FIRENZE
MVSEI

P9-DWY-544

The Museum of
C the Medici
hapels
and San Lorenzo

Introduction by
Monica Bietti
Director of the Museum of the Medici Chapels

Texts by
Antonio Paolucci

s i l l a b e

ISBN 978-88-8347-573-3
© 1999; © 2010 Ministero per i Beni e le Attività Culturali
Soprintendenza Speciale per il Patrimonio Storico, Artistico
ed Etnoantropologico e per il Polo Museale della città di Firenze

A publication by
s i l l a b e s.r.l.
Livorno
www.sillabe.it

managing editor: Maddalena Paola Winspeare
graphic design and cover: Laura Belforte
translation: Anthony Cafazzo, Centro Linguistico Agorà (foreword and introduction);
proofreading by Catherine Burnett
editing: Giulia Bastianelli

photolithography: La Nuova Lito, Florence
stampa: Media Print, Livorno

reproduction rights: Archivio Museo Cappelle Medicee; Archivio Sillabe: photos
Paolo Nannoni, Cristian Ceccanti; Gabinetto Disegni e Stampe degli Uffizi; Casa
Buonarroti Museum; Museum of "Firenze com'era"; Antonio Quattrone; Marco
Rabatti; zenithal shot by Franco Zampetti (pp. 74–75).
The photographs of the Laurentian Library have been kindly provided by its
management.

Reprint   Year
1 2 3 4 5 6 7 8 9 10   2014 2015 2016 2017 2018 2019 2020

Contents

The extraordinary San Lorenzo complex continues to have a multifaceted fascination.

It is the fulcrum of the oldest Christian religiosity, the theater for the Medicis' patronage and commissioning of art, and an excellent system of architecture. The names of Brunelleschi and Michelangelo alone evoke the highest achievements of the Renaissance. It is a treasure chest of artistic works by Donatello and Filippo Lippi, Verrocchio and Bronzino and countless other artists, and an ark of knowledge has been collected in the Laurentian Library. It houses a treasure of sacred art, including precious vases collected by the Medicis in the fifteenth century. But even more than that, it is the pulse of one of the most vital neighborhoods in the historic center, despite the transformations it has experienced and those currently underway.

Antonio Paolucci's text, illustrated with beautiful photographs chosen for this occasion, guides the reader through various places revealing their meaning and value, which time has not changed. The Laurentian citadel is rooted deeply in the very principles of strength and permanence that, in my opinion, have their underground and secret fulcra in the pillars that sustain and contain the vestiges of the Medici family: the celebrated remains of Cosimo Pater Patriae, *whose tomb rests within the pavement at the centre of the nave in front of the high altar, and those of his parents, Giovanni di Bicci de' Medici and his wife Piccarda de' Bueri, whose tombs are above the crypt in the Old Sacristy (designed by Brunelleschi). The tombs of Cosimo's parents serve as the central element in the room, where a collection of precious sacred objects worked in gold is displayed.*

The introduction by Monica Bietti, director of the Museum of the Medici Chapels, gives her account of projects recently completed and others in progress: the successful restoration of the grand ornamental stone surface in the Chapel of Princes, the creation of a new elevator and restrooms for the public, research in the burial vault during the Progetto Medici, *the exhibits, research and publications. With the* Opera Medicea Laurenziana, *the parish and the library, the Superintendency is able to preserve a complex which is unique in the world, and which this guide reveals in its varied magnificence.*

Michelangelo,
The suit of armour of Giuliano de' Medici,
duke of Nemours,
detail. Medici
Chapels, New
Sacristy

Cristina Acidini
Superintendent for the Historic, Artistic and Ethnoanthropological
Heritage and for the Museums of the City of Florence

Introduction

Monica Bietti
Director of the Museum of the Medici Chapels

Since the San Lorenzo complex includes the basilica, the library and the museum, this guide, which is a reprint of the concise, thorough edition written by Antonio Paolucci in 1999, is still relevant, and in fact today this relevancy is further confirmed by the up-dated parts of its text.

So at the publisher's request for a new edition, the previous one being out of print, the question arose as to which would be the best direction to follow to provide the public with useful tools for a enjoyable visit. Given the changes and innovations being implemented in the museum, it was thought advisable not to draw up a new guide ex novo, but to update the previous one where necessary, leaving the publication of a new text and new pictures of the Museum until renovation has been completed. A number of things have changed since 1999. There have been a number of additions to the patrimony (acquisitions, donations, finds), and modifications have been, and are still being, undertaken to bring the Museum into line with the provisions of safety laws and with the indications in the Bill issued by the Ministry for State and non-State Museums. Additional studies are being prepared for publication and research is being carried out that will provide for new, more in-depth knowledge of the San Lorenzo Museum and its patrimony.

In the meantime, this brief introduction will give an account of the changes implemented during the past years and those still in progress, emphasizing only the most significant aspects for an updated tour of the complex.

View of the San Lorenzo complex

Liborio Bracci (carpentry),
Pietro Pertici (intaglio),
from a design by Ferdinando
Ruggieri, *Model of the Chapel
of Princes*, wood, 1740.
Museum of the Medici
Chapels

Perhaps not everyone is aware that one of the museum's main deficiencies concerns the entrance and exit, both positioned inside the great doorway opened in the mid-19th century in Piazza Madonna degli Aldobrandini. Efforts were made to remedy the problem up to 1978, and during the search for a practical solution a "secret" room was found, which we then discovered to be Michelangelo Buonarroti's hiding place in the period around 1530, when the Medici returned to power after a short but intense Republican period. This room is described in the guide, which also illustrates some of the beautiful drawings the great artist made during this period of isolation. A video will now allow visitors to view this hidden, inaccessible place – the steep, narrow stairs do not allow access in accordance with safety standards – while other information in two languages support tours of the rooms and the museum, and also provide facts about the on-going restoration of the Chapel of Princes.

To make this brief note, which outlines the new developments, useful, I will follow the order of a tour of the museum, reserving the necessary additions to the chapter on the treasure of San Lorenzo, on which studies have advanced in the past years and which has been given a new display layout.

In the description, therefore, I will start from the crypt, from which one enters the Museum. Built with lowered vaults and supported by large pilasters in *pietra serena*, it houses the remains of the Medici grand-dukes, placed there in 1857 on the wishes of Leopoldo II of Lorraine, and display-cases containing a part of the San Lorenzo Basilica treasure, kept in the

Vincenzo Meucci,
Dome, *Florentine Saints in Glory* and *The Four Doctors of the Church*, frescoes, 1742

museum since 1945. This is a selection, renewed over time, of extremely precious reliquaries commissioned by the Medici between the 15th and 18th centuries, which can also be admired on the floor above in the sacristy on the left side of the Chapel of Princes. Also on view is a model of the crypt itself, made by Liborio Bracci in 1740 according to plans drawn up by Ferdinando Ruggieri, appointed by Anna Maria Luisa de' Medici to restore the San Lorenzo Basilica and complete it with a new bell tower, and the dome of the Chapel of Princes. Vincenzo Meucci, on the other hand, frescoed the central dome of the transept with *Florentine Saints in Glory* and *The Four Doctors of the Church* in 1742.

The great bronze sculpture portraying Anna Maria Luisa, the last Medici, was donated to the museum in 2004. Shown seated and austere as she gazes pensively towards her tomb, the Electress is an appropriate, significant presence in this place to which she devoted all her energies from the time when, following the death of her brother, Gian Gastone, last Medici Grand-Duke of Tuscany in 1737, she became heir to the family's patrimony, which had to be protected and defended against the greedy hands of political successors. Indeed, it was the princess who conceived and stipulated the so-called 'Family Pact', which tied the Medici patrimony to the State and ensured not only that it remained in Tuscany, but would continue to enrich the then-Grand-Duchy, which she saw as a destination for outsiders attracted by the immense artistic patrimony commissioned and collected by her family over three centuries.

The bronze statue of this great woman, to whom we owe an immense debt of gratitude, was created from the clay model that Alfonso Boninsegni had entered in the competition organized by the then-mayor, Gaetano Pieraccini, in 1946, and was donated to the museum by the sculptor's heirs.

The crypt also houses temporary exhibitions dedicated to the Medici family on themes that draw on finds, research, centenaries and anything that can be tied to the Medicean site par excellence. This choice has its origins in the so-called 'Medici project', a paleopathological, archaeological, historical and artistic-historical study that has involved the Universities of Florence and Pisa, the Superintendence and other Institutes since 2003, and which has led to the discovery of significant aspects of the lives and habits of the grand dukes and their families. Above all, it also led to the finding of both 'Gian Gastone's crypt', the deep underground area that nowadays can be seen on request, and the treasure that was placed in his tomb at the time of his death. These funerary accoutrements, which include two pure gold medals by the grand-ducal goldsmith, Louis Siries, and other devotional objects and symbols of the

11

Grand duke's power that were to accompany him after death, are now displayed in the museum, further enriching it historically and artistically.

On the floor above, in the Chapel of Princes, an incredible mausoleum where the semi-precious stones and rare marbles used have ensured its beauty has remained intact, we find temporary exhibitions but also, and above all, the magnificent end result accomplished by Ferdinando de' Medici when he called upon the most famous master stone craftsmen from Rome and created the Galleria dei Lavori (workshop) in Florence, which is still active today in the Opificio delle Pietre Dure. A tour of its museum is a fitting complement to the enthusiastic, interested tourist's visit.

In the New Sacristy, improvements are envisaged with regard to the illumination and the renovation of the plasterwork as a result of the cleaning of the marble walls. Restoration work

View of the New Sacristy and the Bell Tower from the dome of the Chapel of Princes

has been completed on the coffered dome, which Michelangelo, inspired by the Pantheon, had envisaged with stucco decorations – never completed – on the inside, and covered outside with terracotta shingles and crowned with a temple-shaped lantern in Carrara marble surmounted by a gilded polyhedron with a cross on the apex. This polyhedron has now been substituted with a copy, and the original will shortly be visible in the small room to the right of the Sacristy altar.

Other works, that are already under-way, will attempt to remedy the museum's main deficiencies such as the previously mentioned problem of the entrance and exit, the bathroom facilities, the total lack of rooms reserved for personnel and museum activities, and the unsuitable location of the bookshop. During the work being carried out to install a lift to "reach Michelangelo", a late-Roman mosaic and other objects pre-dating the construction of the San Lorenzo Basilica were found. Services and educational and public spaces are in the planning stage, as well as the possibility of adding areas of great importance and interest to the museum tour, such as the crypt containing the funerary monument dedicated to Cosimo I the Elder *Pater Patriae,* commissioned by his son Piero in 1477 and executed by Verrocchio. The monument is an enormous, solid pilaster on which the chancel of the San Lorenzo Basilica and the Medici dynasty itself are figuratively founded, linked to the church above by the light which filters into the crypt through brass grilles and by the consummately simple and elegant neo-roman motif in porphyry and green and white marble. Demanding, challenging but necessary works that together with the long and exemplary restoration of the Chapel of Princes will cause some disruption to visits in the immediate present, but bring undoubted advantages in the near future.

The Museum of
the Medici
Chapels
and the San Lorenzo complex

Antonio Paolucci

Before entering the Museum of the Medici Chapels one must first get to know and understand the larger monument complex within which it is located and of which it forms an integral part. This is because the Museum of the Medici Chapels is a museum like no other. It had no need of architects to design it. It is simply a piece of the Basilica of San Lorenzo which has been transformed into a State museum only in relatively recent times.

Access to the museum section of the Basilica is through the entranceway in Piazza Madonna degli Aldobrandini, near the apse of the large church.

Just like in any museum, say the Uffizi or the Accademia, you stop by the ticket counter, have your ticket stub torn on the way in, and later, upon conclusion of your visit, you leave. But if on the way out you feel you have been in a museum like any other (like the Uffizi or the Accademia), then it means that the visit has been in vain.

In vain, because the essential point has been missed, which is that the Museum of the Medici Chapels, before being a State museum whose timetable and prices are fixed by law, is first and foremost, the Church of San Lorenzo.

It is in this – in being *San Lorenzo* – that its historical peculiarity and appeal resides. It is for this reason, therefore, that before entering the museum one must understand or, at least, have a conscious awareness of the greater monument of which the museum is part.

The San Lorenzo complex

My advice is to, first of all, to have a stroll round the perimeter of San Lorenzo, now surrounded by the bustling and picturesque market. It will become immediately clear that San Lorenzo is more than just a church. It is almost a city within a city, teeming with history, grandiose as much for its structural complexity as its size.

Its origins coincide with that of the Christian era. It was the year 393 when the Bishop of Milan, Ambrose, consecrated the church dedicated to the martyred Saint Lawrence. In those years Florence was called *Florentia*, and its inhabitants spoke Latin and only partly professed the Catholic faith. During the time of Saint Ambrose, the original

Perspective chart of the complex, called "della Catena", 1470, detail. Florence, Museum of "Firenze com'era"

20

church of San Lorenzo, which no longer exists, was a small building located on the outskirts of the Roman city. Back then, no one would have imagined its future development.

The good fortune of the church began about thousand years later, when in 1418, Giovanni di Bicci de' Medici tackled the task of radically enlarging and renovating the sacred building. The rise of San Lorenzo coincides, therefore, with that of the Medici, who had their house in the same quarter of the city.

Just a short walk from San Lorenzo (at Via Cavour 1), stands one of the most celebrated monuments of the city – the building that belonged first to the Medici and then to the Riccardi family, Michelozzo's masterpiece and a model of 15th-century civil architecture.

In this building – which today houses the Prefecture – lived Cosimo and Lorenzo the Magnificent, before the family became the reigning dynasty over Florence and the Grand Duchy and transferred their official residence to Palazzo Vecchio and then to Palazzo Pitti. These changes of residence did not diminish the Medici's sense of fondness and patronage for their church; on the contrary, over the years, it became ever more steadfast and intense.

San Lorenzo: the favoured parish and church of the Medici for over three hundred years, their palatine basilica and their mausoleum. It is this historical destiny that explains the building's size, its international fame and the richness of its artistic heritage.

For three hundred years San Lorenzo was the official church of the Medici. It was here that the lords of Florence and Tuscany celebrated the weddings, baptisms and funerals of their dynasty; here they attended the great ceremonies of State, and here they buried their dead.

The Chapel of Princes, an integral part of the museum (which we take up later), was their funeral chapel, destined, in the gelid and magnificent glory of its semi-precious stone, to receive the mortal remains of the reigning grand dukes.

The Medici-Riccardi building, Florence, Via Cavour

The Basilica

After strolling round the large building, a pause at the front is well worth the while.

The façade is austere, rough, crossed by horizontal stone lines in relief whose purpose was to bear the marble facing that was never carried out. It is clear that the façade of San Lorenzo is testament to a work interrupted. Originally it had been designed to support a grand architectural project, which however never saw the light of day. Michelangelo was to be the façade's architect.

The many drawings, the vast collection of written works and the wooden model conserved in the Florentine museum of Casa Buonarroti serve to give us an idea of the grandness of Michelangelo's design.

Unfortunately, the vicissitudes of history and politics kept the project from ever taking form. In 1520 the contract was rescinded, and what should have been the masterpiece of Michelangelo the architect, entered forever into the limbo of unrealised dreams.

View of the presbytery roof and the naves of the Basilica of San Lorenzo

Over the centuries, many talented Italian professionals (Pasquale Poccianti in the 19th century, Cesare Bazzani in the early 20th century) proposed

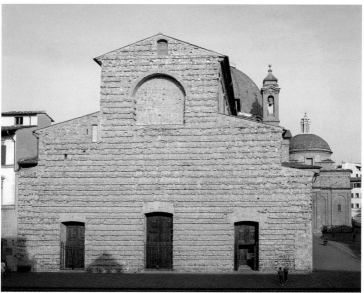

Wooden model of the façade designed by Michelangelo for San Lorenzo, Florence, Casa Buonarroti Museum

Façade of the Basilica of San Lorenzo

architectural solutions for San Lorenzo's façade. Fortunately, they all came to naught – none could hold up against Michelangelo's. The rustic severity of the unfinished façade is preferable to any pretentious, and inevitably inadequate posthumous renovation.

Together with Michelangelo, the other guardian genius of San Lorenzo is Brunelleschi. This great architect has left his imprint throughout the whole building. It was he who conceived of the church as so vast, so rational and so harmonious. Filippo Brunelleschi, avant-garde architect of early 15th-century Florence, was charged by the Medici family with radically restructuring the old church. He succeeded in finishing the Old Sacristy, completed in 1428 (the date inscribed on the lantern dome); he planned the renovation and directed the work until 1446, the year of his death. The remaining work was carried out by his students, especially Antonio Manetti, who was to become his continuer, heir and biographer.

THE INTERIOR

Entering the Basilica today, you will get the impression of a vast, luminous and melodious expanse. Neither the neo-classical additions of Paoletti (the main altar) nor the academic, neo-renaissance ones by Giuseppe Baccani (1860) have been able to obscure the majesty of Brunelleschi's spatial concept. By virtue of its centuries of Medici patronage, San Lorenzo is a church rich in outstanding works of art. It is unlikely that the visitor will ever find enough time to admire them all with due attention.

Filippo Brunelleschi, Interior of the Basilica

Rosso Fiorentino,
The Wedding of the Virgin,
oil on wood panel, 1523

For example, by the second altar on the right, there is a panel (dated to 1523) by Rosso Fiorentino, which deserves a visit in its own right.

It depicts *The Wedding of the Virgin* and would require reading Giorgio Vasari to fully appreciate the "ease of its execution", the tender iridescence of the robes, the "extreme grace of the women", the "bizarre and capricious" coiffures,

Desiderio da Settignano,
Tabernacle, marble,
circa 1461

"the bizarre semblance of the old men's heads" and the "sweet and pleasant air" of the women and *putti*. Tenderness and outlandishness, joy in colour and a fearful and restless testimony to visible beauty – these are the elements that dominate this admirable stage in the artist's career, set along his path like an authentic moment of grace before the dramatic formalism of his last period. It is regrettable to devote only a quick glance to the marvellous panel by Rosso Fiorentino and the refined *Tabernacle* by Desiderio da Settignano (circa 1461), currently located at the back of the right-hand wall.

There are two places, however, within the Basilica of San Lorenzo that demand longer and more thorough scrutiny.

These are: the space at the end of the nave where two bronze pulpits by Donatello face each other, and the Old Sacristy, a masterpiece by Brunelleschi and Donatello together.

The pulpits and the Old Sacristy are more than just celebrated works of art, they are compulsory pages in any text, even the most schematic, on the history of Italian civilisation. One cannot claim to know the Florentine Renaissance in its most heroic stage, unless one has stood, at least once in a lifetime, before these pulpits and inside this Sacristy.

Donatello was already an old man, ill and near death, when he accepted Cosimo the Elder de' Medici's commission to carry out the two bronze pulpits for the church (circa 1461–1465).

Although he was helped by many pupils and collaborators, the dominant stylistic features, distinguished by an expressionist and dramatic conception of sacred history, can be attributed wholly to the maestro. The other, anti-classical and visionary spirit of the Florentine Renaissance emerges with particular force in these superlative masterpieces by Italy's greatest sculptor after Michelangelo.

Donatello,
*Pulpit "of the Passion":
Agony in the Garden*

Donatello,
*Pulpit "of the Passion":
Crucifixion, Lamentation*

To the left of the nave, looking towards main the altar, is the pulpit called "of the Passion", because the bronze bas-reliefs depict the sacrifice and death of Jesus Christ as narrated in the gospels. The scenes, in chronological order, recount to us: the *Agony in the Garden*, *Christ before Pilate and Caiaphas*, the *Crucifixion*, the *Lamentation* and the *Deposition*. Its posterior part was completed in the 17th century with wooden bas-reliefs of the *Flagellation* and *Saint John the Evangelist*.

Donatello,
Pulpit "of the Resurrection":
Descent into Limbo,
Resurrection, Ascension

To the right of the nave, opposite and symmetrical to the other, is the companion pulpit called "of the Resurrection". The bas-reliefs represent, albeit not in rigorously chronological order, the most important evangelical episodes following the death of Christ: the *Entombment*, the *Descent into Limbo*, the *Resurrection*, the *Ascension* and the *Pentecost*. Behind it is the relief with the *Martyrdom of Saint Lawrence*, signed by Donatello and dated 1465. The Gospel that Donatello narrates in the bas-reliefs of Saint Lawrence is disconcerting in its modernity and tragedy.

Opposite and above:

Donatello,
Pulpit "of the Resurrection":
Entombment, Pentecost,
Martyrdom of Saint Lawrence

On the following pages:

Donatello,
Pulpit "of the Resurrection":
Descent into Limbo,
Resurrection

Of the many possible examples, I would like to provide some detail on one in particular: the right-hand pulpit contains the *Resurrection of Christ*, apogee of the whole narrative.

Traditional iconography has always depicted this episode of Christ's life as one of victory and glory. This is not so with Donatello. Christ emerges exhausted from the sepulchre, leaning on the crossed standard, as if ascending an agonising stairway. He is still enveloped in the swathes of his shroud. His numbed and spent body and far-away countenance are laden with death. He appears as if caught in the death throes from which he is still emerging in order to carry out a painful duty. There is no trace of glory in the resurrection of Donatello. His Christ looks like the unfortunate victim of a concentration camp, finally able to leave – Christ leaving the tomb almost furtively, oppressed by the misery of the human condition, so aching and lonely that one would think he is doubting the usefulness of his own resurrection, while at the same time, compelled to it by the fatality of a love which no living being deserves. This Christ is an important key to understanding the pessimistic religiousness of the sculptor and his highly dramatic vocation.

Agnolo Bronzino, *Martyrdom of Saint Lawrence*, fresco, 1565–1569

At the end of the nave, before turning into the left transept of the church, we can see the mannerist depiction of the *Martyrdom of Saint Lawrence*. This work was executed by Bronzino between 1565 and 1569 on a commission from Grand Duke Cosimo I. It was evidently conceived in homage to Michelangelo's work in the Sistine Chapel with an architectural composition in the background embodying neo-Raphaelesque classicism.

The Old Sacristy

At the end of the left transept a door made of various precious types of wood leads through to the Old Sacristy, which was constructed by Filippo Brunelleschi on a commission from Giovanni de' Medici and completed in 1429.

This work is exactly what the manuals and literature of art say it is: a perspective box, a geometric poem, the architectural manifesto of the Renaissance, the conscious recovery of ancient rhythms and measures.

The entrance to the
Old Sacristy, 14ᵗʰ century

41

Around you they glide, the serene, white walls and clear pilasters, angular shells of *pietra serena* and lithesome capitals.

Stand in the centre of the Sacristy and contemplate the dome from directly below, observing the radial ribs irradiating outward from its centre, like a harmonious wheel. The impression is of something very vast, very old and very solemn, like the Pantheon in Rome or Saint Sophia in Constantinople.

Donatello, *Saint John bringing Drusiana back to Life*

Donatello, *The Agony of Saint John*

Donatello, *Saint John on the Island of Patmos*

Donatello, *The Assumption of Saint John into Heaven*

Opposite page:

Donatello and school, Lunettes with bas-reliefs representing *Saints Stephen and Lawrence* and *Saints Cosmas and Damian*

Inside Brunelleschi's well-defined framework unfold the polychromatic stuccoes by Donatello, friend and rival of the great architect.

In the upper register Donatello placed the images of the four Evangelists within tondos and episodes from the *Life of Saint John* in the pendentives.

The Medici Saints, *Cosmas and Damian, Stephen and Lawrence*, occupy the lunettes beside the apse over the bronze doors, also modelled by Donatello with figures of the Martyrs and Apostles facing each other.

Donatello, *Door of the Martyrs*

Donatello, *Door of the Apostles*

Andrea del Verrocchio,
Funerary Monument to
Piero il Gottoso and Giovanni
de' Medici, 1472

To understand how much this site represents the perfect synopsis of Florentine artistic civilisation at its zenith, one need only consider that the Old Sacristy also holds Andrea del Verrocchio's

47

Giuliano d'Arrigo,
known as Pesello (attr.),
*Small dome of the apse of
the Old Sacristy depicting
the celestial hemisphere*

absolute masterpiece, the *Funerary Monument
to Piero il Gottoso* (the Gouty) *and Giovanni
de' Medici*, inaugurated in 1472, and that the small
dome of the apse contains a singular symbolic rep-
resentation of the Florentine sky, dated July 4 of
the year 1442 and attributed to Giuliano d'Arrigo,
known as Pesello.

Here, the two spirits of the Renaissance are both
represented on a higher level: the perspective and
rationality of Brunelleschi, the expressionism
and anti-classicism of Donatello, together with
the refined and intellectual manner of Andrea
del Verrocchio, Leonardo da Vinci's maestro who,
in his early *Annunciation* (in the Uffizi), in fact,
refers precisely to Verrocchio's sarcophagus in
the Old Sacristy.

The patronage of the Medici hovers over all, like a
guardian spirit, seeking to make this old Sacristy
a place of excellence – the mirror and emblem of
their aesthetic and cultural values.

Filippo Lippi, *Annunciation*,
wood panel, 1437–1441

The moment has now come to leave the church. First, though, a worthwhile stop in the Martelli Chapel, next to the Old Sacristy. At the altar is an *Annunciation* executed on wood panel by Filippo Lippi between 1437 and 1441.

It is one of the foremost works in the history of Renaissance painting. The perspective vision, applied ten years earlier by Masaccio in the Brancacci al Carmine Chapel and theorised by Leon Battista Alberti, finds one of its most poetic expressions here. The discovery of the 'real' in the certainty of quantifiable space, scrutinised to its furthest reaches – this is the secret of Florentine painting in the years of Filippo Lippi, Beato Angelico, Domenico Veneziano and Piero della Francesca. Consider the bottle, half-filled with the clearest of waters (symbolising Maria – the vessel of purity), and you will understand that what you have before you is one of the truest and most beautiful still-life paintings in the history of European art.

Now observe carefully the bottom of the painting: the garden, the vine, the white architecture

Opposite page:

Donatello (attr.),
Sarcophagus of the Martelli Family, marble, circa 1455

50

which act as frame to the annunciation.

Look at it again and again, because when you leave the church and enter the cloister (the entrance is to the left, facing the façade) you shall find yourselves, as if by magic, immersed in a similar atmosphere of musical harmony and composed serenity.

Before leaving the Martelli Chapel it is well worth taking to moment to look at the "woven basket" tomb of Niccolò and Fioretta Martelli, a little-known masterpiece from 1455 attributed to Donatello which complements Lippi's painting on wood on the altar with naturalistic simplicity.

The Cloister and the Laurentian Library

The cloister is very large and formed by a two-storey loggia: an arched lower one and the architraved upper one, both resting on small Ionic columns.

This is architecture transformed into rhythm and poetry, just like the lower part of the painting by Filippo Lippi we have just seen.

Observe the very well-kept garden, with boxwood hedges and an enormous orange tree in its centre, and you will get the impression of being inside Sandro Botticelli's *Primavera* (Spring) in the Uffizi.

The city of Florence still reserves surprises of this sort.

Once the church and the cloister have been visited, one must at least have a glimpse at the Library which is part of the San Lorenzo complex.

Bartolomeo Ammannati,
The stairway to the
Library, 1559

Opposite page:

Michelangelo, Vestibule of
the Library

Today the Laurentian Library is an Institute of the Ministry for Arts and Culture. Renowned the world over, it contains Italy's most important collection of ancient books and codices. There is no scholar of ancient history or human sciences that does not know and has not visited this place at least once.

The core of the Library is made up of the books collected by the first Medici, guided by the advice of humanists such as Vespasiano di Bisticci.

It was Pope Clement VII de' Medici who, in 1523, ordained that the family library find a permanent place within the walls of San Lorenzo.

Michelangelo was charged with designing the hall to hold it.

For more than ten years Buonarroti continued to supervise the undertaking, from design to construction. When he moved to Rome in 1534, Giorgio Vasari and Bartolomeo Ammannati continued the work, adhering to the maestro's plan.

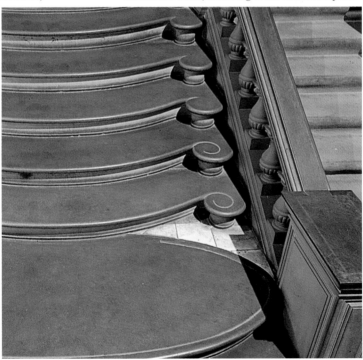

In 1568 the Library was finished. Although it was Medici property, it was freely open to specialists of any circumstance and origin.

Entering the Library (from the Brunelleschi cloister) is a moving experience. First of all, there is the Vestibule (also called the *ricetto* or reception hall), marked by the dichromatic play between the white of the plaster and grey of the *pietra serena*. The atmosphere has been defined as one of "sculpted architecture". Indeed, Michelangelo treats twin columns, pillars, friezes, tympana and mouldings as plastic elements, like lines of force under mutual tension.

That which for Michelangelo, the sculptor, is a duel – hand-to-hand combat with the marble slab – here becomes a competition with space, a space that Buonarroti's spiritual energy dominates with dramatic effects. Passing through the *ricetto* and ascending the stairway that Ammannati carried out in 1559 after the maestro's design, we come to the Library.

In the same way that the Uffizi is the archetype of all museums, the Laurentian Library is the

archetype of all libraries. It is unlikely that there is a 16th-century atmosphere anywhere in the world that has conserved such a high level of excellence and equally great formal homogeneity.

Here everything is original, everything has been carried out according to Michelangelo's original conception: the glass showcases with the Medici crest, the monumental wooden benches, also designed by Michelangelo, the red and yellow terracotta floor, designed by Buonarroti's pupil, Niccolò Tribolo.

The desks maintain the stands with the codices arranged in their original positions. Upon leaving this monumental hall of the Laurentian (for many it is no longer a place of study, but a museum in its own right), the visitor will have realised that the

Opposite page:
Details of the terracotta
floor of the Library
reading room

Aristotle, *Logic* (Plut. 71.7;
c. 2*r*), 15th century

State Institute overseeing the Library is entrusted
with the safe-keeping of some of the most important manuscripts in the world: the Byzantine
version of Justinian's *Pandects*, Horace's *Odes*,
annotated by Petrarch, the *Divine Comedy* with
the annotations of Giovanni Villani, Aristotle's
Logic, illustrated with the miniature portraits
of Cosimo the Elder and Piero de' Medici, the
Codex known as "Biadaiolo", along with many
other documents fundamental to the history of
Western civilisation.

The Museum of the Medici Chapels

Now, having visited the church, the cloister and the library, we can move on to the entranceway in Piazza Madonna degli Aldobrandini to visit the museum known the world over as the Medici Chapels. After taking measure of the vastness and complexity of San Lorenzo, which has over the centuries been, yes, a church, but also a library and an artistic and cultural laboratory *par excellence*; after having understood the symbolic, exclusive and eminent role that the Medici wished to impart to that which was, at the outset, their parish church, it will not be difficult to understand the singularity of this museum, different from any other in Florence or Italy.

Upon entering the Museum of the Medici Chapels, the visitor should be conscious of the fact that it is, above all, a memorial site: the place destined to harbour the mortal remains of a family of rulers. In this sense, this museum can be compared to the Capuchin Crypt in Vienna, the Habsburg mausoleum, San Lorenzo de El Escorial, where the Spanish kings rest, or with the Church of Saints Peter and Paul in Saint Petersburg, which houses the tombs of the Romanovs.

The Medici Tomb is made up of two parts: the so-called Chapel of Princes and Michelangelo's New Sacristy. The visitor must pass through the former to get to the latter, thus inverting the chronological order, but following the path set down in the middle of last century (1855) with the renovation of Piazza Madonna degli Aldobrandini and the inauguration of the current entrance which, through the crypt, leads to two Medici sites *par excellence*.

The Chapel of Princes

The Chapel of Princes is a grandiose structure, oversized even with respect to the vast dimensions of San Lorenzo.

If you observe the layout of the Basilica, you will realise that this octagonal structure covered with white marble and *pietra forte*, crossed by small perimetric apses and illuminated by vast windows, was conceived as a true central-plan church leaning on the presbytery and choir of the Basilica to which it is linked. However, it emerges as a building in its own right and, as such, distinct and unique in Florence's urban fabric and city skyline. Looking at Florence from above it is evident that, in terms of architectural marvels, the dome of the Chapel of Princes (designed by Ferdinando and completed – except for the apical lantern – by Giuseppe Ruggieri in the early 18th century when the Medici dynasty was already failing), is second only to the dome of the city's Cathedral, Santa Maria del Fiore.

Once the Medici became grand dukes, the legitimate sovereigns of Florence and Tuscany and therefore a reigning family, they desired a building that would be the visible sign of the glory and longevity of their dynasty. The contour of the Chapel of Princes stands out in the city skyline as a symbol of their power, destined to outlast the death of each.

The life of a grand duke is fragile and brief, like that of any human being, but the power that each sovereign represents and exercises, by divine right, during the time granted on this earth, this power, is forever.

Such is the substance of the message contained within the Medici mausoleum. In order to give form to this concept, at the same time both religious and political, the lords of Florence did not hesitate to spend prodigious sums to cover their tombs with semi-precious stones – materials as incorruptible and eternal as they are cold and valuable.

The ideas of Death and Power in the time of Catholic Absolutism find their most splendid manifestation in the Chapel of Princes. Only the Mausoleum of the Spanish kings at El Escorial has the ability to convey analogous impressions.

Proposal for the decoration of the second order of the dome of the Chapel of Princes, 17ᵗʰ century. Florence, Gabinetto Disegni e Stampe degli Uffizi

It is significant that the dimensions and form of the Chapel of Princes were conceived by a cadet of the Medici family, Giovanni, himself an architect, as well as man at arms.

In 1602 a competition was decreed for the Chapel design. Buontalenti and Silvani both entered projects, but the one preferred was that of Matteo Nigetti who, inspired by Giovanni's ideas, was charged with the work up until 1650.

The work proceeded slowly throughout the century, draining the ever dwindling financial resources of the ebbing Grand Duchy.

It was Anna Maria Luisa de' Medici, last heiress of a dynasty destined to disappear with her, who imparted the decisive impetus to the work. She lived to see the arched dome completed, but the lantern and ribbing that would echo the dome of Santa Maria del Fiore were never carried out.

The model, still preserved in the museum, is testimony to the project that, with the death of the last of the Medici line in 1743, was to be definitively abandoned.

Anna Maria de Medici demonstrated moving fidelity to the dynastic dream of her ancestors in the years that saw the extinction of her family and the State already handed over to the succeeding Lorraine dynasty. Let us recall this extraordinary woman, whose modest tombstone was placed precisely at the entrance of the museum, near the right-hand stairway leading to the upper floor. Let us recall Anna Maria Luisa de' Medici because it was she who, with the famous family pact of 1737, bound the succeeding foreign dynasty to the perpetual conservation in Florence of the artistic patrimony of the crown and its accessibility to the public. It is to her that we owe a debt of gratitude that today the Piero della Francescas, the Botticellis, Raffaellos and Titians, the pride of Florentine museums, are not in Vienna or Prague. Meanwhile, the Lorraine did not forget the Chapel of Princes.

In 1791 Ferdinando III had the crypt rearranged as a burial ground.

Later (1828–1837) the neo-classical painter Pietro Benvenuti decorated the dome with a series of frescoes dedicated to Biblical stories, from Genesis (*Creation*, *Original Sin*, *Abel's Death* and

Pietro Benvenuti,
Dome of the Chapel
of Princes, depicting
stories from the *Old and
New Testament*

Deluge) to the life of Christ (*Birth*, *Crucifixion* and *Resurrection*) and the *Last Judgement*. The octagonal ring nearest the lantern-skylight is divided into hexagons, each of which is decorated with images of the four Evangelists and the four Prophets.

Actually, the perpetual work on the Chapel of Princes was destined to last even up to very recent times. Of this, let it suffice to say that the main altar panels were inlaid with semi-precious stone of various ages and origins during the years immediately preceding the last world war and that the floor, entrusted to the Opificio delle Pietre Dure during the 1870s, was concluded only in 1962.

At first sight, the Chapel of Princes gives the impression of a vast and harmonious place, larger than it actually is.

The regularity of the typically Florentine, central-plan octagon remains buried, but not contradicted by the magnificent splendour of its interior decoration.

Mannerist and Baroque aesthetics in Florence and Tuscany have always depended on a classical framework, unveiling its rational spirit.

Augusto Betti, *Dinner at Emmaus*, 1853, semi-precious stone intarsia panel set in the altar in 1938

Above and on the following page:

Grand Ducal manufacture, *Decorative panels*, 14th-century, semi-precious stone intarsia panels set in the altar in 1938

The grand dukes wanted a mausoleum that would allude to the majesty of the Pantheon, to the great dimensions of Roman monuments, but in order to communicate immortality – the immortality of the individual soul and the immortality of the dynasty – they used the most splendid and imperishable materials: marble and polychrome granite, porphyry, Barga red, Corsican green, jasper, alabaster, quartz, lapis lazuli, coral and mother of pearl.

The Opificio delle Pietre Dure, founded in Florence in 1588 by grand duke Ferdinando I as a State workshop in the service of the court, is still active throughout the national territory as an Institute specialised in the restoration of stone and art work. Over the centuries it has dedicated a great part of its activities to the decoration of the Chapel of Princes.

Immense wealth and many generations of skilful artisans have been involved in this costly enterprise, comparable to the operations of a large-scale goldsmith's.

Inside the octagon covered with polychrome marbles and semi-precious stones six niches open up, inside which are the cenotaphs of the Medici grand dukes who rose to the throne of Tuscany. All are present, except the last, Giangastone. Each niche contains an urn bearing the ducal crown.

Above, in the frieze that runs the perimeter of the chapel, in big capital letters of semi-precious stone intarsia, are the names of each of the sovereigns resting in the sepulchres below.

Each niche was destined to hold the bronze statue of a fallen sovereign; at least, this was the intention of those who commissioned and designed the tomb. However, only two figures were ever carried out, that of Ferdinando I, the work of Pietro and Ferdinando Tacca (1626–1631), and the other, of Cosimo II, executed by Pietro Tacca alone (1626–1642). Both are masterpieces of 17th-century Florentine sculpture.

The sovereigns are depicted full-length facing the viewer, holding the symbols of autocratic power (crown and sceptre) and dressed in the ermine mantle of Grand Master of the Order of Saint Stephen.

They have perished, and the mausoleum consigns their memory to eternity, but it is as if they were

Pietro Tacca, *Cosimo II,* 1730s–1740s
Pietro and Ferdinando Tacca, *Ferdinando I,* 1730s–1740s

Coats of arms of Tuscan cities adorning the lower level of the Chapel of Princes

still alive. In fact, the sculptors have depicted them in the flower of life and at the height of their institutional activities, showing that the sanctity and immortality of dynastic power are transmitted, intact, from one sovereign to the next by legitimate right conferred directly by God.

Because the Chapel of Princes, even more than a place sacred to the memory of the deceased sovereigns, is the sanctuary of the Grand Duchy, it represent it in effigy and celebrates it in the dazzling glory of semi-precious stones.

Indeed, the octagonal baseboard surrounding the room's lower wall contains the shields of the sixteen most important cities of the State: Pienza, Chiusi, Sovana, Montalcino, Grosseto, Pisa, Massa di Maremma, Siena, Fiesole, Pistoia, Florence, Borgo Sansepolcro, Volterra, Arezzo, Montepulciano and Cortona. At the time, each of these cities was an Episcopal seat. Taken together, they represent the Tuscan people. Only Lucca is lacking because at the time it was an independent republic. The presence of these city shields within the mausoleum signifies the whole of the State paying homage to the deceased sovereigns.

Their position at the foot of the statues and the grand duke's sarcophagi is the visible emblem of the unanimous submission of the Tuscan cities to the autocratic power of the reigning family.

In the Chapel of Princes, the idea of Power in the time of absolutism and the Counter-reformation thus takes the shape of an extraordinarily suggestive teaching parable.

The New Sacristy

Leaving the Chapel of Princes, one must of course enter Michelangelo's New Sacristy, the heart of the museum and an irresistible attraction for the thousands of people that visit it each year.

The New Sacristy is a relatively small room, and yet, such is its celebrity and the echoes of Michelangelo's presence, that the impression is one of breadth, like a space expanding toward an indefinite spiritual measure.

Just like the Sistine Chapel, no visitor to the New Sacristy can escape the impression of having entered one of the grand places of the Spirit: places that appear wide and almost incommensurable, despite their true dimensions.

But before taking on the art, and the myth, of Michelangelo, some historical background and elements of basic iconography are called for.

Lantern of the New Sacristy

Silvio Cosini, *Trophies of arms*, marble, circa 1525–1530

We enter, then, into the New Sacristy through a straight aisle containing two 'heroic' *Trophies of arms*, sculpted in marble by Silvio Cosini, a native of the Tuscan city of Carrara and collaborator of Michelangelo, and likely intended for the funeral monuments of the Sacristy itself.

The Sacristy was created by will of Pope Leo X de' Medici, who wished, with funeral memorials of suitable splendour, to honour his ancestors: his father, Lorenzo, and uncle, Giuliano, together with his brother Giuliano, duke of Nemours, and nephew Lorenzo, the duke of Urbino.

It was another Medici Pope, Clement VII who took up the enterprise and made it a reality in 1520, entrusting the works to Michelangelo. Buonarroti, architect and sculptor of the New Sacristy, laboured on it for nearly fourteen years; the most dramatic years, not only of his life, but also of those of Pope Clement, the Medici family and the city of Florence, itself.

In fact, this historical period was to see the Looting of Rome (1527), the siege of republican Florence (1530), which Michelangelo defended in his capacity as military architect, and the definitive return to the power of the Medici, backed up by the Spanish armada.

When Michelangelo moved definitively to Rome in 1534, the Sacristy had not yet been finished, although the architecture and sculpture were almost ready.

It was Giorgio Vasari and Bartolomeo Ammannati (1554–1555) who, by order of Cosimo I, brought Michelangelo's work to a worthy conclusion.

The architectural envelope that harbours the Medici tombs is very simple: a cubic space topped by a hemispheric dome.

The reference is evident to Brunelleschi's Old Sacristy, symmetrical to it in the layout of the Church, but it is obvious to all who have seen it, that Buonarroti rendered a tense and dramatic personal interpretation of the atmosphere there. As in the lobby of the Library, we could once again say that we are in the face of "sculpted architecture". Once again, the space is tackled as a rival from which to wrest intensely expressive messages. Against the white-plastered walls, the architecture of Michelangelo sets its clear framework in *pietra serena*, forming grooved pilasters, cornices, mouldings and windows fitted with triangular tympana – elements typical of the structural and ornamental architecture of the time.

However, Michelangelo at times uses conventional language to express radically new topics. His structures are tense forces contradicting the calm harmony of surface and space that we found in Brunelleschi's work.

We enter the New Sacristy as into a tense force field. Michelangelo has transformed the model of Brunelleschi into a dramatic theatre to exalt and intensify the drama of the sculptural groups.

The drama unfolds in the lower part of the Sacristy, where the sculptures are located. The room here is covered with marble on three of its sides – a rhythmic chain of twin pilasters, niches, festoons and cornices with their mascherons.

Michelangelo wanted to impart a heroic foundation to his contemplation of death.

As the New Sacristy is a mortuary chapel – a fact often ignored by visitors – the dominant topic is the immortality of the individual soul. For Christianity immortality is a dogma of faith. God's mercy welcomes all to eternal peace, commoners and Medici princes alike.

One of the Sacristy's four walls, the one without marble facing, contains the Virgin group with Saints Cosmas and Damian. This depicts Paradise, the ultimate hope of all believers.

The *Virgin and Child*, located in the centre, was executed by Michelangelo in 1521. What strikes one most is the melancholy face of this sweet, yet powerful Virgin holding her Herculean son tight to her breast, as if presenting his sacrifice on the Cross. It conveys a sense that she wants him all for herself. The gesture of possessive love is imparted to her body by a 'serpentine' modulation which painters and sculptors have for centuries tried to reproduce in countless ways.

The *Saints Cosmas* (to the left) and *Damian* (to the right), guardians of the Medici family, reflect the aesthetic models of Buonarroti in both their style and heroic positions. They are the work of his pupils and closest collaborators: Giovan Angelo da Montorsoli (*Cosmas*) and Raffaello da Montelupo (*Damian*).

At the Virgin's feet, in a simple marble base to which they were transferred in 1559 from the provisional tomb in the Old Sacristy, lay the mortal remains of Lorenzo the Magnificent (d. 1492) and Giuliano de' Medici, killed in 1478 during the Pazzi conspiracy. The monument that, in Michelangelo's original project, should have commemorated them, was never carried out.

Michelangelo, *Virgin and Child*, 1521, detail

Wall of the New Sacristy with the *Virgin and Child* between *Saint Cosmas* and *Saint Damian*

Giovan Angelo da Montorsoli, *Saint Cosmas*, circa 1537

Raffaello da Montelupo, *Saint Damian*, 1531

Michelangelo,
*Giuliano de' Medici,
duke of Nemours,*
1525–1530 (?)

The main characters of the New Sacristy, there-fore, are not the most well-known lords of Florence, those spoken of in history books, but two minor characters, two cadets of the Medici house: Giuliano, duke of Nemours, and Lorenzo, duke of Urbino. The first (d. 1516) was the third son of Lorenzo the Magnificent and brother of Pope Leo X, the latter (d. 1519) was son of Piero il Fatuo (the Vain), and was the inspiration for Niccolò Machiavelli's *The Prince* and father of Alessandro, first duke of Florence. Both were destined to die young; both dedicated their brief existence to a career in arms.

Two captains of illustrious name, destined to great success, die in the prime of life. The world mourns

Michelangelo,
*Lorenzo de' Medici,
duke of Urbino,* 1531–1533

their premature disappearance and meditates on
destiny, which cuts short the promise of glory in its
prime; it meditates on all-consuming time and the
immortality promised in the heavens to all believers, but which noblemen and the virtuous (and the
young captains are both) also attain on this earth.

It is the task of art (in this case, the art of
Michelangelo) to deliver memory to immortality. This is, in short, the philosophy that inspired
the tomb of the Medici in the New Sacristy of
San Lorenzo.

Now, let us observe closely the two sepulchral
monuments placed one opposite the other.
To the right is the statue of Giuliano, duke of
Nemours. He is dressed as a military leader, bare

Michelangelo,
Tomb of Giuliano de' Medici,
duke of Nemours

headed,dressed in armour and holding the staff of command. He is seated, as if holding audience to his officials on the eve of battle; face turned abruptly right, as if imparting orders or making a sudden decision.

Man is action and thought. This is what moralists and philosophers have taught us. Combinations of the active and contemplative forge the distinctive character of each one of us. Duke Giuliano represents the active life; Lorenzo, just opposite him, instead symbolises reflection and meditation. The right balance between action and thought, both represented by the two captains one opposite the other, give fullness to human nature. It is of great importance to understand that the Medici Tombs seek, not only to celebrate two illustrious personages, but also to give form to the conception of man according to the ideas of Plato, theories which Michelangelo shared.

But let us return to the tomb of Giuliano, duke of Nemours. At the captain's feet, spread on the volutes of the sarcophagus, are two allegorical figures. They represent Day (to the right) and Night (to the left).

Day and Night, together with Dawn and Dusk occupying analogous positions on the tomb of Lorenzo just opposite: these are figures of time, coursing inexorably through the sky and consuming everything in their wake, the life of common mortals as well as the glorious destinies of eminent captains.

Night is represented as a young and athletic woman sleeping with her recumbent head resting on her right hand, while her muscular body is depicted according to the artificial model of mannerist 'antithesis'. Upon her and to her side are the symbols of night: the crescent-moon diadem on her forehead, the dream-inducing poppies at her feet, and then the owl, lord of darkness whose grinning countenance alludes to the nightmares populating the dreams of men.

Day is a masculine figure whose face is unfinished. In symmetry to Night, he echoes the same body posture, but his gaze is toward us in an act of dominion, raising his unfinished head as if to

Michelangelo,
Tomb of Giuliano de' Medici,
Night

represent the indistinct and blinding splendour
of the sun as it traverses the heavens.

We are accustomed to imagining the sculpture
of Michelangelo in black and white. An attentive
study of Day and Night reveals that, to the contrary, the artist wanted to impart 'colour' to his
marble, achieving it through application of particular treatment to the various surfaces. Thus,
the polished body of Night glows with a cold, lunar
clarity, while the rough surface of Day, in the mass
of rough, amberish marble, almost seems to preserve the light and warmth of the sun.

It is fascinating to examine closely the technique
of Michelangelo, a sculptor aiming at the attain-
ment of pictorial-chromatic effects. Nowhere else
will you have the chance to do this as well as in the
New Sacristy. Sometimes, the chisel penetrates
the marble as if it were living flesh, and deep shadows thicken to create dramatic fields of dark tension. Other times, the marble surface is brought
to mirror clarity, so that the forms fill with a melodious shimmer. Yet other times, the surfaces are

Michelangelo,
*Tomb of Giuliano de' Medici,
Day*

traversed by a vibrant, satin hatching.

One cannot but marvel at the sight of the bent leg of Night, as brilliant as a crescent moon, as pure as a river pebble smoothed over by millions of years of flowing water. And what to say, faced with the incomplete head of Day, observing the chisel strokes that riddle it with dramatic shadows, the etchings of the *gradine* chisel that glow like the painter's brush strokes!

It is not hard to understand why the sculptures of the Medici Tombs have over the ages fascinated critics and poets to the point that all that the writings on these masterpieces could fill a library.

It is not only the supreme quality of the artistic result that fascinates, but also the philosophical and symbolic meanings that envelop the sculptures, together with the poetic images they conjure.

Michelangelo himself, in a famous sonnet written after the political and military affairs that had led to the fall of the Florentine Republic, gave voice to "his" Night, evoking words of the bitterness and melancholy which in those days afflicted him:

Michelangelo, *Night*, details
Michelangelo, *Day*, detail

'Dear to me is sleep, and more so, if it is of stone,
while the grief and shame persist;
to not see, not hear, is to me great fortune;
but wake me not; for God's sake, speak softly.'

Michelangelo,
Night, detail

Michelangelo,
*Tomb of Lorenzo de' Medici,
duke of Urbino*

The companion sepulchre dedicated to Lorenzo, duke of Urbino, was carried out during the last years of Buonarroti's stay in Florence, between 1531 and 1533, when the Medici had already returned to power thanks to Spanish military might, and the dream of a democratic republic shared so passionately by Michelangelo had definitively dissolved.

While Giuliano, the imperious and strong-willed captain, represents the active life, Lorenzo symbolises reflection and meditation, Man's other fundamental nature. The term "pensieroso" (pensive), generally applied to this melancholy warrior in the literature, is thus perfectly suited to the subject represented.

Like Giuliano, Lorenzo is also seated, armed and therefore prepared for action, but with a reflexive and meditative demeanour. At his feet, symmetrical to the Day and Night of Giuliano's sarcophagus, we find two more allegorical figures, Dawn and Dusk, signifying once again the rhythmic flow of time.

Just as the extremely temporary states Day and Night impel one to the active life, Dawn and Dusk, transition moments almost of waiting between the light and the darkness, are better suited to the temperament of this pensive captain.

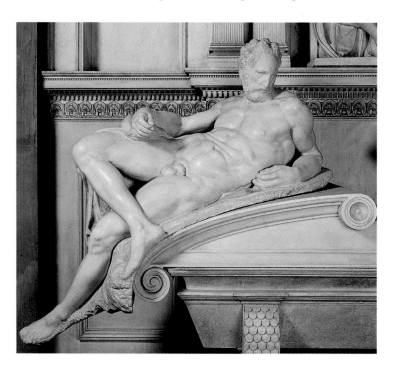

Michelangelo,
Tomb of Lorenzo de' Medici,
Dawn

Dawn is a large female figure who seems to be waking slowly from a dream, stretching her limbs and shaking off the torpor of the night. Twilight, on the other hand, is a male nude at rest, the unfinished head slightly inclined, as if cowed by the travails of the dying day.

Time, divided into its four fundamental parts unceasingly repeated under the sky (Day, Night, Dawn and Dusk) is, therefore, lord of the Medici Tombs.

It is all-consuming time that subjugates the glory of the captains, whose temperaments (action and thought) embody the very nature of man. As we have said, however, this philosophy of history must come to grips with immortality. The immortality of art is clearly manifest, but there is also a transcendent vision which unites Platonic and Christian philosophy – the immortality of the individual soul.

Michelangelo, *Dawn*, details
Michelangelo, *Dusk*, detail

Many visitors to the New Sacristy do not realise that they are inside a Catholic chapel.

The glorious captains of Michelangelo, though looking very much like heroes from Plutarch or Roman Caesars, are set in a transcendent Christian dimension. It is significant that the gaze of both are turned towards the image of Virgin Mary – for Christians "the refuge of sinners" and "Heaven's gate".

The Sacristy also contains an altar for celebrating the Eucharist. The two monumental, sculpted-marble *Candelabra* located at the ends of the altar were designed, though not executed, by Michelangelo. The one to the right was sculpted by his pupil Silvio Cosini, while on the left is a later copy carried out in 1741 by Girolamo Ticciati.

Opposite page:
Silvio Cosini,
Candelabra on right, detail

Ornamental repertories

We could not leave the New Sacristy without first considering the ornamental repertoires.

Generally, visitors do not pay them much heed – so engrossed, almost hypnotised as they are by the great statues – emblems of the heroic duel with absolutes and history, of which the Sacristy (like the Sistine chapel) is a mirror and image.

And yet, in these ornamental repertoires, Michelangelo unfolds extraordinary visual fancies that seem to breathe life into these apparently conventional images.

In the metopes, the ram's skull strikes out at us like a metaphysical object.

In the altar candelabra, the acanthus leaves unfurl at the edges like carnivorous plants, and the lions' paws claw in spasmodic tension. The laurel festoons have an unsettling weight and vitality, the overlapping scales on the sarcophagi and the false windows resemble the armour of monstrous animals, looking like they are about to move at any moment.

The ribbons and festoons dart like serpents, the capitals allude to swarming corollas of marble, hyper-real demon heads, like the masks of Japanese theatre, coat the warriors' armour.

Almost another world, a night world populated by grotesque images and, at times, by melancholy and horror; this is the decorative universe that Michelangelo invented for the mausoleum of the Medici. Innumerable artists of his and succeeding generations have treasured this formidable ornamental Atlas set forth by him in the New Sacristy.

In 1978 the academic world was shaken by a discovery that seemed clamorous at the time.

During restoration works in a small basement located on the left-hand side of the New Sacristy a number of charcoal drawings were found on the walls. Paolo Dal Poggetto, the person responsible for the important finding, attributed the drawings (some of such high quality as to justify the possible authorship of Michelangelo) to the presence of Buonarroti in San Lorenzo during the critical days of the end of the siege (1530) and the return to power of the Medici.

We know that Michelangelo was a friend of the rector of the Figiovanni Basilica, and cannot exclude the basement's having served as a temporary refuge for the artist. He was in fact, an eminent member of the anti-Medici party and military engineer for the Republic during the assault and, for this reason, may have feared the political revenge of grand duke Alessandro.

Such revenge was, however, never taken, because once in Florence, not only did the Medici not harm the great sculptor, but rather, always demonstrated extreme respect and high regard of so illustrious an 'enemy', protected by the Pope and already renowned in Italy and throughout Europe.

However, the story unfolded, the drawings conserved in the basement of the Sacristy, though not visible to the public for the lack of properly regulated

Michelangelo (?), Wall drawings in the New Sacristy basement, charcoal access, are a repertoire of 16th-century graphics of great interest because of their undoubted link to the work done by Michelangelo at San Lorenzo.

Stairway to the "secret room" or crypt of the New Sacristy

Works in gold

At the outset, it has been said that the Medici Chapels is a wholly singular museum.

As a visitor, you will realise this the very instant you pay your admission. In fact, the entrance fee is the sum of two different charges: the first and higher of the two is levied by the State Administration, the other, more modest one, goes to the *Opera Medicea Laurenziana*, that is to say, the lay organisation that for centuries has administered and safeguarded this great church, seeing to its many management and maintenance needs. The close symbiosis that ties the Museum to the Basilica is also carried over in their administrative and accounting aspects.

On the other hand, (and herein lies the justification for the additional charge), the church is a concrete part of the State museum and offers a superb anthology of its most precious decorations for the admiration of visitors.

For the historical reasons we have mentioned (a palatine church under the auspices of the reigning family, official site of celebrations of State), San Lorenzo has over the ages benefited from the lavish donations of Florence's most prestigious *ateliers* and the Opificio delle Pietre Dure.

These are reliquaries, liturgical vases and altar decorations that were presented to the faithful on important occasions from the tribune purposely designed by Michelangelo on the inner façade of the Basilica.

There was no illustrious or intellectual personage from Italy or Europe, who during a visit to Florence did not request the privilege of visiting the Treasure of San Lorenzo.

This extraordinary collection of applied arts is presently conserved partly in the Basilica, under the care of the ecclesiastical authorities, who have recently arranged an exemplary display in the lovely underground areas of a rich selection, partly in the Museo degli Argenti (Silver Museum) (the late-antiquity, Byzantine and Sassanian vases originally owned by Lorenzo the Magnificent and nationalized in the Lorraine era are famous), and partly in the Musem of the Medici Chapels.

The latter are the objects that visitors can admire

Florentine manufacture, *Standard of Leo X*, silk, gold, silver, early 16ᵗʰ century

in crypt and the sacristy to the left of the Chapel of Princes. There are objects that alone would be the pride of any great Italian or European museum: a pearl-encrusted *Mitre*, a *Standard* made of silk and gold in the fabric and decorative 'greccia' motif which made Florence and the Medici's fortune in Europe, and the gilded chased silver *Pastoral staff* bearing an image of Saint Lawrence (San Lorenzo) in the round, hidden inside the curve of a laurel branch, all gifts of Pope Leo X.

There are rare reliquaries in rock crystal, gold and silver worked in Florence, but also of Oriental manufacture and belonging to Lorenzo the Magnificent. There are others, commissioned by the Medici family, in precious metals and also in semi-precious stones from the grandducal workshops and others of German or Flemish manufacture

Florentine manufacture,
Mitre, embroidery with
pearls, early 16th century

Venetian manufacture,
*Reliquary of Saints Cosmas
and Damian*, rock crystal,
gilded silver and enamel,
15th century

Opposite page:

Massimiliano Soldani Benzi,
Reliquary of Saint Casimir,
silver, 1687

Giovan Battista Foggini,
Reliquary of Saint Sebastian,
semiprecious stones, cast
and gilded bronze, 1714

Giuseppe Antonio Torricelli,
Reliquary of Saint Emeric,
semiprecious stones and
ebony, 1717

brought as gifts by foreign princesses related to the Medici.

The Treasure of San Lorenzo bears testimony to the great artists working at the court: Giovan Battista Foggini (*Reliquary of Saint Daniel, Reliquary of Saint Sebastian, Reliquary of Saint Sigmund*), Massimiliano Soldani Benzi (*Reliquary of Saint Casimir, Reliquary of Saint Alexis*), Giuseppe Antonio Torricelli (*Reliquary of Saint Emeric*); extraordinarily elegant, precious objects perfectly complemented by those exhibited in the new Basilica Museum, making a unique, unforgettable collection of absolute excellence. Admiring the liturgical ornaments on display, visitors will also understand that San Lorenzo's centuries of religious history are the fundamental, indispensable reason for the fascination of this singular museum.

Index of artists and relative works

Medici Coat of Arms,
Dome of the Old Sacristy

Medici heraldic symbols, detail of the
terracotta floor of the Laurentian
Library reading room

On the following page:
Michelangelo Buonarroti, *The Owl*, detail
of *Night* in the *Monument to Giuliano
de' Medici, duke of Nemours*